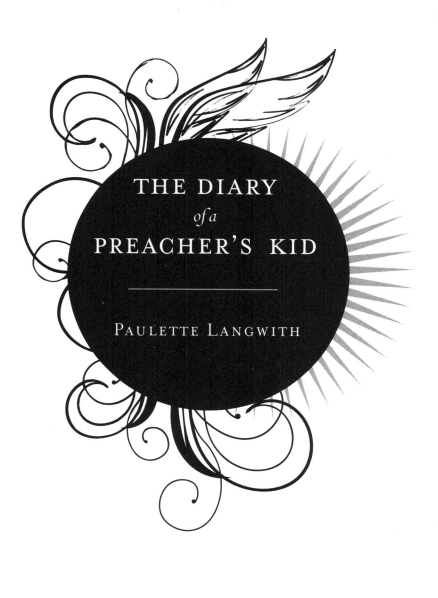

THE DIARY
of a
PREACHER'S KID

PAULETTE LANGWITH

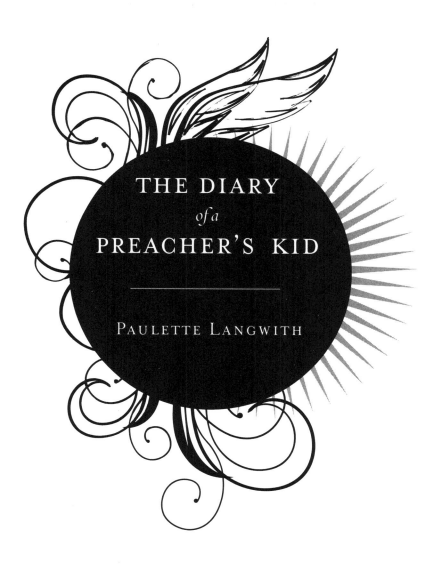

THE DIARY
of a
PREACHER'S KID

PAULETTE LANGWITH

CREATION
HOUSE
A STRANG COMPANY

THE DIARY OF A PREACHER'S KID by Paulette Langwith
Published by Creation House
A Strang Company
600 Rinehart Road
Lake Mary, Florida 32746
www.strangbookgroup.com

Unless otherwise noted, all Scripture quotations are from the King James Version of the Bible.

Design Director: Bill Johnson

Cover design by Justin Evans

Library of Congress Control Number: 2009934259
International Standard Book Number: 978-1-59979-919-3

First Edition

09 10 11 12 13 — 987654321
Printed in the United States of America

I dedicate this book first and foremost to God for giving me the grace I needed to forgive myself—and to my Phoenix First Assembly family for keeping me with the most open loving arms.

Graham, you have always believed in me, and I thank you for always being the unconditional reminder of how much God loves me.

Finally, I thank my mom and dad for trusting me to write this story and for always making me feel like I could do anything.

Daddy—you are my hero, and mom—you are the most amazing woman I know.

Contents

Introduction

I HAVE KNOWN FOR several years that I needed to write this book. I have honestly done everything in my power to keep from writing this book because I had an enormous fear about what I would have to reveal about myself in order to do it. Simply put—I did not want to be judged by anyone. So, I must warn you to be prepared for some harsh truths, reality, and outright failure in the Christian journey we affectionately term as "perfect."

Even in all my godliness and holy surroundings, I was soon broken and exposed to the harsh realities and consequences of life. Unfortunately, I was not prepared to handle any of them. A dab of mascara was a far cry from the events that would take place in my life once I turned twenty-one.

This is the hard part. I now ask you to understand, at the risk of hurting anyone who thought different of me, that God did allow certain circumstances to take place so that I could have this moment with you right now. This book will be brutally honest because I truly believe that God does not want me to share a "censored" truth. He wants someone—even if only one person—to understand just how much God will bring you through.

In one deep breath, here it is. I was married and separated. Revenge afforded an adulterous affair; I wound up pregnant, had an abortion, reunited with my husband, separated, and finally divorced. The next ten years I spent searching, running, and facing consequences to my sins, never realizing that God had a plan. And now I am sharing this with you in *The Diary of a Preacher's Kid*.

chapter one

Growing Up

I was raised in a Pentecostal Christian home. My father was born in the Promised Land (North Carolina), and my mother was a French Catholic waiting for the revelation that earrings were the "sure ticket to hell." All joking aside, the movie *Footloose* was obviously based on a true story. Fortunately for me, I also had church members to keep me on the straight and narrow. Having a French mother came with genetic traits that most deemed as glamorous facial features, including dark eyelashes, which were occasionally vigorously rubbed by righteous church members for any evidence of mascara—an abomination to God (at the time).

I attended public schools all of my life and was nicknamed "Churchie." I would love to say that the nickname came simply from being a witness, but I stood out for other reasons too. I would say it was more of a fashion statement; I wore dresses and skirts everyday. I never wore pants, or makeup. I didn't mind being called Churchie. In fact, I considered it an honor to be a light in such a dark world. I was able to remind those around me that cursing and French kissing were indeed the *new* ticket to hell.

I graduated from high school and soon left for a Christian

college in the Bible Belt Buckle—the campus where Christ was King! Oddly enough, attending the school did not make Christ Lord of your life. You still had to have a relationship with Him. We had mandatory chapel three times a week, and at that time we were not allowed to wear pants until after 5:00 p.m. As the semesters passed, God began to "lighten up" a bit. I'm still not exactly sure what happened, but eventually we could wear pants to class, but not to chapel—and then we could wear pants to chapel too, but absolutely *no shorts*!

While some of you may be reminiscing about your college days, wondering how you would have survived, I felt safe. It was a lifestyle I was comfortable with—something I knew about. Don't get me wrong, there were the occasional crazy nights—being late for curfew, driving out to a bigger city to dance a few songs (of course, it was so early that hardly anyone was there). We had to be back at the dorm by 11:00 p.m., and if we were an hour away that meant we left by 10:00 p.m. The pseudo rebel was on time once again!

I have a wonderful mother and father, one brother, and two sisters. My brother is ten years older, one sister is nine years older; then there was me, the baby, until my little sister came long ten years later. What were my parents thinking? Needless to say, we were all on pins and needles when my little sister turned ten years old.

As far back as I can remember, I have always been a preacher's kid. My father served twenty years in the Air Force, but I only know him as a minister. I remember living in Limestone, Maine, and shoveling snow to get out of the house. My first memory of a spiritual moment was in first grade. Apparently, I was so on fire for God that I won my first grade teacher to the Lord (or maybe my parents did and just gave me credit). I also remember living in Portsmouth, New Hampshire, where our house was on the first floor and the church was on the second floor. My father had decided to take a "hurting" church. A hurting church can mean many things—hurting people or hurting financially. In this case, it was both. In fact, the people were hurting so much they weren't coming to church, which simply means there was no offering. No offering means...well, I really don't know how we made it during that time. I distinctly remember eating a lot of grilled cheese.

My parents were under so much stress to try to provide for a church and provide for a family with no income. I can't imagine the stress my parents must have been feeling, but I do remember what it looked like. On a rare occasion that we had green beans my mother reached into the boiling water and threw a handful of green beans at my dad. My father walked away and went into his prayer closet. My dad felt like a failure. He needed God to show him that he was in the right place. Christmas was around the corner and although we had food (grilled cheese), we still had a hurting church. It seemed like moments later there was a knock at the door. A woman had no idea why she was there, but handed my dad a check for $75. We had Christmas that year!

After a year of barely making it, my dad felt led to move to New Mexico. He was appointed to another hurting church, but this time it was different. My dad was deter-mined to fulfill a vision God had given him. In fact, he named the church Vision Church of God. He went back to school at forty-two years of age with his G.I. bill (which was a benefit from being in the military for twenty years), got a degree in bricklaying, and built a Sunday school annex. As defeated as he may have felt in New Hampshire, God was going to restore him in New Mexico. I was in the third grade now.

My dad's church grew tremendously. The church started with ten (including us) and grew quickly to almost two hundred. My dad also grew our family (this is where my aforementioned little sister was born). We had eight years of a prosperous church with my father's growing and pressing vision. During this time, my parents poured into the church and the people of the church.

I remember on one rare occasion that I was sick and had to miss school. I loved school. My dad was at the hospital, visiting members of the congregation. My father came back home to check on me, and I vomited on his three-piece suit. I don't know if any of the members knew that the preacher's daughter was home ill, and to be honest I'm not sure they cared. Everyone needed my dad—even me. If you are that church member that demands a visit from the pastor, don't be offended. You may truly need your pastor, but I just needed my dad.

Even in success, stress continued to brew in our home. My mother missed her family in France so much. We had financial ups and downs and simply could not afford to go to Europe to visit. As the church grew, so did the financial commitments. To accommodate my father's fluctuating salary, we moved into eight different homes in eight years. No one knew how much my father gave, except his own family. Again, I'm not sure anyone cared. After all, that was his job.

Church members were quick to tell my brother and sisters how to dress, the length of the dress, how to speak, and how to wear our hair. Out of respect we simply nodded and complied with their ridiculous requests (this compliance carried over into college). After walking two miles home from school in the New Mexico sun I had to plead with my mother that I was not wearing blush. She could not risk a member of the church questioning the godly upbringing of her children.

My parents became so concerned with what the church members thought of us that perfection was not an option. I cannot even begin to try to put into words how difficult this situation became. The church was demanding more time of my father, and my mother was faced with the continuous reminder of our imperfections. My mother did not know how to handle the homesickness, the church requirements, and the stress of her children. Her own childhood is not one she speaks of, so I know she did the best she could.

Talking back in our home was as simple as asking, "Why?" I give my parents credit for coining the phrase, "Because I said so." My mother began to live and breathe the scripture "spare the rod, spoil the child." The problem was the rod was defined as whatever was closest—a kitchen utensil, a belt, and even the occasional backhand. She had to break me. She had to break us. Even my little sister was striving to meet these unrealistic expectations. She was acting as most four-year-olds do—inconvenienced by life—complaining about stairs, or food, or lint (who knows). I do know my mother backhanded her so hard she fell into my arms and blood began spewing from her nose. Maybe if we had just been more obedient the consequences would not have been so great. Disobedience was not an option. "Children, obey your parents in the Lord: for this is right."

Please understand, *my mother was not a monster.* She truly was trying to live a godly life commanded by the members in our church. It was just an unobtainable goal.

I looked at my mother with strength and anger in my eyes and told her to hit me—not my sister. My dad said nothing. He had no energy left for us. In fact, when I told him that I was scared—that mom was hitting us really hard—he looked at me and said, "Do you want your mother to go to jail?" I don't know if there was a conversation between my mother and my father, or if God truly intervened. My mother never touched us again.

Before you judge my mother, God has absolutely delivered her from the fear of people, and she is the most amazing woman in my life.

Through it all, we continued as a perfect family, as the church required us to be.

We sang in church (even if we weren't that good), played every instrument available in the church, all self-taught. I started to play the alto saxophone in sixth grade. I believe my brother used to play, and it was my mother's favorite instrument. I learned quickly how to play by ear so I could play in church. On top of everything else, I am proud to say I was a band geek. I loved the band. I felt safe there too. I tried to learn a couple of other instruments, especially where they were needed in the church. When I grew older, I remember my father asked me to play the piano during altar call. I only knew one Christian song, and the other was the theme from Ice Castles. I was very creative.

Today, kids have their own service! How cool is that? I wasn't allowed to write or "play" during church. In fact, during one sermon, my father saw me talking and he stopped his sermon and asked me to come and sit on the front row—definitely not the attention I had planned on that day. My mother was a pro at the arm "pinch and twist." If I wasn't playing the piano for the altar call, I was usually at the altar because of some unforeseen sin somewhere in my life.

Although I am older now, it makes me sad that so many religious folk made it their unintentional calling in life to remove any joy God had planned in my life, the life of my parents, and even my brother and sisters. Although the recovery has taken years and in some cases is "still in progress," it was not God that hurt us; it was people.

The day my mom gave her heart to the Lord a very "spiritual" woman informed her that the earrings had to go. They were earrings that her mother had given her when she left France. It was in that moment, when God had planned to fill her heart with grace, that happiness was instantly replaced with the conviction of men. That dear sister planted the first seed that would steal the joy God had planned for our family.

I consider myself to have grown up in New Mexico. We were there from my third-grade year through tenth grade. I remained extremely sheltered, and that was just fine with me. I struggled with how to manage perfection, school, and family. Although I was only eighty-five pounds as a sophomore in high school, there were a few occasions when I sneaked a Dexatrim to make sure I wasn't dealing with my stress through food. Fortunately I didn't develop an eating disorder, partly because my mom literally forced me to eat a peanut butter sandwich. And although I don't necessarily encourage that method, something snapped for me. I knew I had to find another way to deal with things.

My dad made an announcement to the church: we were going on a vacation! It was our first vacation in eight years. We were going to Europe to visit my mom's family. We flew "Space A" which is a military term for space available. That also means you fly wherever they take you. So it took us a few countries to finally get to France. When we arrived in France, my mom was nervous and anxious. It was even more important to my mom for us to be perfect for her family, possibly something to do with her own childhood. We just did our best with our broken French and communication barriers.

We had a great time as a family—four whole weeks of vacation just us *and* my dad! When we came back to New Mexico something happened. My father had that defeated look again. I truly don't know exactly what happened, but I do know my father made another announcement that Sunday morning. He was resigning as pastor of the Vision Church of God. He resigned from his vision. Even today, that is his one regret. Pastor Tommy Barnett taught a sermon on "The Honor of Wanting to Quit." The only problem was my dad did quit.

chapter 2

Sprechen zie Deutsch?

I FOUND OUT MANY years later that church members had rallied together to let my father know that *they* would tell him what he could preach and teach. They wanted to be comfortable coming to church, not challenged. They wanted to hear about how God loved them, not how His only Son died on the cross—that's too morbid. I don't know if my dad was stunned or needed medication, but his next announcement was that we were moving to Germany. *What? Do we speak German?*

It was now the summer before the eleventh grade. You have to understand that I had an amazing career in the band. In ninth grade, I won outstanding soloist three times in one year, and by tenth grade (which was the first year of high school) I was sitting second chair. On top of everything else, we had just returned from New York to march in Macy's Thanksgiving Day parade. I shook hands with Bo Duke (John Schneider) from the real *Dukes of Hazzard*, for goodness sakes. What in the world would I do in Germany? Oktoberfest? Nein!

Nevertheless, we sold everything we had and began the long "Space A" journey to Germany. My father became the director of the Ministry to the Military Servicemen's Center in Amberg, Germany, an army training facility. My dad has always had a heart for the military, and although he quit his vision, God opened a door where his heart would heal.

There is an incredible thing about having a congregation full of military families: they understand how important family is. In fact, these servicemen would come over to our house to be part of *our* family. The pressure of perfection seemed to dissolve over time. My parents were laughing again, and my mom was close to home. Best of all, these servicemen showered us all with unconditional love. God truly was healing my family. I am so grateful to the many people who blessed us through this time in our lives.

My father had Air Force benefits as a retiree, and although the medical insurance was great, the benefit program did not include the ability for me to attend the American School on Post. Dad decided to home school me. I was soon very ready for this man, whom I had previously missed so much, to start hospital visitation again. I could not function in home school; it just wasn't in me. Did I mention I loved school? My father decided to get an entry-level military job (G4) that would give him the school benefits I so desperately needed.

My little sister was young enough that she was already speaking fluent Birish (Bavarian German) so she attended German school, which was a great benefit to my parents when they had a question on their utility bill!

I had incredible eleventh- and twelfth-grade years at Vilseck American High School. I had wonderful friends who sheltered me more than my parents did until something bizarre happened. It was my senior year in high school on my seventeenth birthday. My mother informed me that my present was on my bed. I walked in my room and saw a cream-colored pair of corduroy pants. I better repeat that—*pants*! I went back out to the living room and told my mom there must be some mistake. Did she accidentally order something for dad? My mom and dad looked at me, smiled, and said, "They are for you." My first pair of pants? What was going on? *I love Germany!*

My dad began to ask for forgiveness and told me that for so many years they had let "people" convict their lives rather than God. No more. God had placed him as the head of the household, and as for him and his house, we would serve the Lord (no matter what we were wearing). I walked into school the next day, and you would think I was naked. Everyone just stopped and stared. My best friend ran up to me and said, "Churchie, do you need a ride home? What happened?" I looked at him and smiled. I had so much joy. I proudly announced, "They were a gift from my mother and father." I didn't even care that they were two sizes too big. *They were pants!* My father and mother had just planted the first seed of joy that God had planned for my life.

You should also know (if you are taking notes), I started wearing makeup and went to my first movie and my first dance! I even quit the band for one semester and went on the drill team, which is a "dance" team. Of course the first song we performed was "Papa, Don't Preach" by Madonna. Still, my senior year had to be the best year of my life at the time. It is amazing the joy that became part of our once defeated

15

family. I also started to date that year. My parents "lightened up" where appropriate. However, when it came to dating, the unsuspecting guy would have to come into the house, meet my parents, explain what we were doing, where we were going, how long the movie would be, etc. I did not mind any of that either. It kept me safe.

I went on a date with someone from high school, and I think all he wanted to do was kiss the church girl. It was two days after my sixteenth birthday. It was true, sweet sixteen and never been kissed! And then it happened, my first French kiss! It didn't seem like the movies, though. Wasn't I supposed to see fireworks? I just remember thinking, "Oh my gosh, am I a bad kisser now?" We broke up, I think, the next day. I was sure I could never date again!

I went to teen camp that summer and met a boy. He was beautiful, tan and just amazing. He did have one flaw for my parents. He had long hair. But it didn't matter; I truly believed that God had made him for me, at least for that summer. We prayed together, walked together, and even had little picnics. I knew he wanted to kiss me, but I didn't dare. I was ruined. My first kiss did *not* win an Oscar, and he would know. He was persistent, so I finally confessed my fear. I have never seen someone laugh so hard. Needless to say, there was a moment, and he became my very, very first kiss. You know—the fireworks kiss. He was such a gentleman. He kept his hands on my shoulder blades and everything. We decided to start dating. He lived about two hours away, but he could drive, and I would be driving soon.

My parents met him, our families met, and it seemed to be

a godsend relationship. Everything was perfect, until about three months later I received a phone call from his mom. She told me that there was a girl that was pregnant, and my "godsend" was the father. I told her she must be mistaken because he was dating me. I did not even understand the concept of "cheating"—amazing, huh?

When I finally put two and two together, which took some time, and an uncomfortable conversation with his mother and mine, I was devastated. How could this happen? How could this amazing first-firework-kiss relationship end so abruptly? I was done dating for a while—a long while. He played football for Ansbach High School, and little did he know that I had friends on the Vilseck football team. It was the day of the big game, Vilseck vs. Ansbach, also known as Paulette vs. teen camp boy. His family was there and came to see me. Little did I know that many, many years later I would see his family again, only to disappoint them with the broken vessel I had become. But that day, they loved on me and then there was *him*. I didn't know what to say, but he picked me up and carried me off the field. He apologized.

We never got back together, although I truly wanted to. I knew I could forgive him. Instead, his best friend asked me out. After several months of mourning, I said OK. He was nice and decent, but he wasn't *him*. I should have never dated him because it was too close to *his* home. He knew I still loved *him*, and I think that is why he tried to be so many "firsts" for me.

I fought his hands a lot. I never told my parents for fear they would have him arrested—literally. In fact, I tried to break up with him a couple of times, but he would call my mom. I ended up going to my senior prom with him because my mom asked me to. After it was all over, and he realized we were through, he proposed to me. He told me that my mom and dad had given him permission. I hesitated and said yes. After all my parents had done for me my senior year, if this was really what they wanted for me, I had to say yes. We walked into a restaurant, and I saw my mom's face. She didn't know! She didn't know at all! When I returned home, I put the ring in the box. I couldn't believe he had done this to me. My first proposal and my parents didn't even know!

The summer of my senior year, I was debating on colleges. I was trying to decide between an all-girl school in the east, and a Christian school in Tennessee. Meanwhile I was spending time with my friends and trying to figure out what to do with the ring in the box. I had gone to visit a good friend of mine from high school whose father had just been transferred back to the States. He told me he was going to miss me, and then he kissed me goodbye. This was more than a "friend" kiss—this one had fireworks! Now I knew what to do with the ring in the box: send it back! Churchie was *not* ready to get married. It was truly just a kiss—an amazing kiss, but just a kiss.

chapter 3

BACK TO THE U.S. OF A.

WITH JUST WEEKS before a college start date, my father made a phone call to a good pastor friend, and Tennessee was the place for me! When I got there, I was definitely a fish out of water. Although the strict college rules kept me safe, I didn't know how to react without my parents meeting my friends, making sure I did my homework, and most importantly making sure I was being spiritually fed. I could stay up late, eat junk food in the cafeteria, and embrace the "Freshman Fifteen" tradition. It was amazing.

At college, I didn't stand out as much. Everyone was "Churchie." All the girls wore dresses, and pretty much everyone was a virgin. I was actually blending in except for one little thing. I had never in my life had a tan. So the nice pale green tinted skin was definitely a shocker for the Tennessee southerners. Luckily, my new roommates introduced me to baby oil and iodine—a wonderful mixture of sun poisoning in a bottle. I got it and I got it bad. I peeled for months, and I even had to miss class. At least I was learning the "important" things: why big hair is a necessity, piggyback perms are the only perms, and four shades of eye shadow is a very sophisticated approach.

A former beauty queen lived in my dorm, so under expert tutelage I began to look like a pageant queen with layers of "godly" makeup. My parents still have this picture of me hanging up in their home with the largest hair and darkest makeup you have ever seen. My husband (Graham—who is introduced later in the book) laughs every time he sees it.

I became interested in boys, and Tennessee was a wonderful state for cute ones. I dated a few different boys, and learned the art of making out. I had a group of friends that I hung out with, including an African-American boy. I guess you could say we were "talking," which means we were interested in more than friendship. According to the concerned counsel I received, this relationship could damage my reputation. In this area of Tennessee, being unevenly yoked also referred to black and white relationships. I would love to say that I rose above it, but I was still too impressionable to make my own decisions. I told him we could not see each other, nor could we be friends. I couldn't risk my reputation. I still don't know whom I was trying to impress. I do know I hurt him in the process.

With all of the reputation guidelines in place, I barely had time for school, and it showed. I came home my first semester from college with a whopping 1.6 GPA. I left for college with a 3.85. Did I even go to class? The important part is I looked good, right? My mom and dad were furious. My parents almost didn't send me back, but I pleaded and begged. I did go back, but knew it would be my only chance to prove myself in my grades.

According to the reputation police, I would be lucky if even one "white" guy wanted to date me again. Luckily, one white guy was brave enough to revert me back to "same-race" dating. He was pre-med, so studying was also part of my dates. He was fun and definitely helped me focus on my schoolwork. I'm not complaining as I did bring my grades back up, which was one less worry on my plate.

I know it seems like I have dated quite a few boys by now, but remember, I was never intimate with them, so it was not that difficult to date someone else.

The next couple of years I studied hard and was invited to join a Social Service Club, which in laymen's terms could be considered a sorority, but we actually did do wonderful things for our community and our school. The hazing consisted of buying a goldfish, being blindfolded, and then swallowing it. Okay—it wasn't really a goldfish—it was a slice of tomato (clever, I know!)

I started dating another boy and dated him for almost two years. I really loved him. He was a virgin, too, and there was never any pressure. We truly just had fun meeting for biscuits and gravy in the cafeteria (when he would show up) and walking me to class. He really was a good boy. I have to be honest; at one point I thought we should lose our virginity to each other because I knew I would never meet anyone like him (that is, a male virgin), but I also knew we couldn't have a life together. Everyone always says you need to marry your best friend, but he truly was just that—a best friend. It was a very difficult breakup for the both of us, but I knew God would take care of us.

I quickly jumped back into the social scene at college (newly single) and ready to meet Mr. Right. We had a Sadie's Hawkins event—you know, where the girl asks the guy out on the date. The only catch (perhaps a Tennessee catch) is that there is a big "chase." If the girl "catches" the boy, he has to pay for the date. Seems harmless enough, right?

I broke my collarbone. Although my roommate tried desperately to take care of me, I decided to withdraw from school that semester and head home.

chapter 4

HOME SWEET HAUSEN

I HAVE TO ADMIT it was wonderful to be home with my family back in Germany. My mother is probably the best "nurturer" I have ever met. I rested for a few days (long enough to no longer need painkillers) and began to heal quickly. I was excited to head back to school, but apparently I had some dating to do, military style.

I attended chapel with my parents and there I saw him—the most amazing chiseled appearance of a perfect man. He was like Gaston from *Beauty and the Beast*—only more beautiful and extremely intelligent. He was a graduate of West Point and lieutenant in the army. He spoke five languages, one of which was French, so my mother fell in love before I could. He asked me out on a date, and I have to tell you it was like a fairy tale. Did I mention he was beautiful? We saw each other as often as we could, and I really started to like him. I mean, how could I go back to college boys after dating this guy?

One evening we were going to dinner, but we had to swing by his place first. My mother didn't mind that I spent time with him alone, and I soon discovered why. I was in the car and he looked over at me and said, "I just want you to know I don't want your virginity." I was shocked! I replied in horror, "How did you know I was a virgin?" He interrupted me with the words every twenty-one-year-old virgin dreads to hear, "Your mother told me." I wanted to scream. I felt the heat rush to my face. I even had a moment of arrogance as I thought, but *everyone* wants my virginity. I wasn't thinking about giving it to him, but I did want him to at least want it…I mean, isn't that what every guy wanted?

We continued to date a few more weeks. I still enjoyed being with him, but things were different now. I think I became very self-conscious of the clearly drawn boundaries that my mother had so gracefully drawn. Soon enough I got the "Dear John" talk; actually, he said, "I'm leaving for Desert Storm and it doesn't really make sense for you to wait for me." I said, "OK." That was it. I got home and let my mother know. She was devastated. "You can wait for him!" she cried. I tried to explain that *he* broke up with me.

I tried to date one or two more times before heading back to school, but my mother would have no part of it! In fact, on one date, she locked me out of the house gate. He could not even drop me off at the door. I was so embarrassed! Poor mom, she loved "Gaston."

I learned a lot in those few months being home. I learned that being the church girl was not all it was cracked up to be. I learned that boys (other than the teen camp boy) could break up with me, and I learned that dating could be romantic—fairy-tale-like, if you met the right guy. (Insert theme from *An Officer and a Gentlemen*…)

chapter 5

SCOTTY

I RETURNED TO SCHOOL and I met Scotty. We had the same faith and believed the same things. The epitome of perfectly yoked! Scotty even had his own apartment. Our dates "out" now consisted of renting a movie and making out on the couch. I think I even had a wine cooler (yes, I said *wine cooler*). I remember my willingness to offer him everything I could possibly give, even my virginity (I'll show you, Gaston!).

After a long meaningful relationship consisting of two weeks, and being a twenty-one-year-old virgin, I did *it*. I had sex (at least I think that is what it was). It was nothing like I imagined. There were no candles, no roses, and no silk sheets. I drove home the next morning wondering what I had done. Did I look different? Would my roommate know? Was there now a scarlet letter pinned on my back that I couldn't see? And of course, there was my mother's voice, "If you wear white at your wedding, you better deserve it." My life was ruined.

I felt no one else would want me now. I was no longer pure. One moment of emotional weakness forced a hopeless journey to begin. It was not a journey God intended, but rather my own free will that paved the way. I would "guilt" myself into abstinence only to give in once every three months. I knew in my heart of hearts that Scotty was not the one for me, but he had my virginity! I had to make him keep me. God gave me so many signs, yet I ignored them, faced with the consequence of losing my virginity. I had to make him love me. God *had* to make this work.

As I begin to describe in detail the next few years of my life, it is important for you to know that this is how *I* felt, driven by pure desperation to become righteous in the eyes of God. Scotty was going to fall in love with me *and* marry me whether he wanted to or not. The amazing thing is that I put all of this pressure on him over "virginity," not pregnancy. The harder Scotty ran, the more I chased him.

Six months into our now "forbidden fruit" affair, he was several hours late to meet me, and I was very concerned. Cell phones were not the common commodities they are today. So, I just waited. He showed up at my door reeking of cologne and mouthwash. *What's that smell? Oh, marijuana. Isn't that illegal? Now that should be a sure ticket to hell! Nice try, Scotty, but I will not have you leave me! I will simply forgive you.* Yes, that's it. I would forgive him. I had to; he had my virginity!

For the next year, I did just that—I forgave him. Finally, on February 29, 1992, the night of my proposal, my MRS degree was in sight.

I would love to tell you how I was swept away during a romantic candlelight dinner, finding an engagement ring in the bottom of a glass of very berry wine cooler, but again, no. I was at his apartment. I think he just finished taking a shower. He walked out into the living room and said he had a surprise for me. I do love surprises. In fact, if you ask Scotty to tell the story, he apparently had a romantic proposal planned, but he said the magic word *surprise*. So, I begged and pleaded (as any virgin-less girl would, seeking her own righteousness) to give me the surprise right now. He asked me to close my eyes and when I opened them, he was on both knees asking for my hand in marriage. *Yes, yes, yes—now I will become legitimate. Now, I will be made whole once again! I will be righteous in the Lord's eyes!* He even called my father to ask for my hand in marriage. My father told him, "No!" Parents, you do have that right, but just be prepared that we may not listen. Obviously, my dad did not know that this proposal was the salvation I needed.

I finished off my senior year with a beautiful diamond on my hand, and we started marriage counseling. God sent another sign. We were closing our session in prayer, and the minister stopped and said, "Scotty, whatever you are dabbling in, you need to stop." *Dabbling in? What in the world is Scotty dabbling in?* Of course, being the driven fiancée I was, and determined to be righteous in the sight of God and marry the man who had my virginity, I asked. "What are you dabbling in?" He replied, "Oh, I've just been curious about magic tricks and stuff." Magic! Magic was like earrings, a sure-ticket to hell. So I dropped it. Scotty had always been an eclectic soul. He embraced theological discussions and spiritual warfare. *Ummm, hello? I just need to get married here. Stop dabbling and let's get to wedding planning!*

Our wedding date was set for three months after graduation. Although wedding planning can be considered a stressful time, my struggle was with my family. My mom disliked the idea of engagement, much less a wedding. (Wait a minute! Was she still hoping for Gaston?) She chose not to attend my college graduation in protest, if you will. Please don't think that my mother was conditional with her love in any way. I honestly think that somehow she just knew. She had very bad feelings about this marriage. She was just being overprotective, I thought. The MRS degree would be here soon enough! My entire family did come to my wedding, and everything was as it should be. A lot of people held their tongues as to what they really thought.

Then came my big moment with my amazing dress and the walk down the aisle with dad. His heart was full of love for his princess. As the double doors opened with music on cue, Daddy looked at me and said, "Baby, you don't have to do this. We can walk out of here right now!" I was shocked. "What? I'm sorry, Daddy. You must think we are at rehearsal! This is it, for goodness sakes!"

As quickly as possible, I composed myself and took the walk down the aisle. I don't remember the wedding too much, but the reception could have been the party of the year. We had an open bar at a country club. Goodness, people were so excited to celebrate our now biblical union. For many, I am sure there was no memory at all.

We left the reception, and at that point everything changed. I transitioned into my newfound role as a wife. Redemption was upon me. Church was a requirement, and he was going to be the leader of the home whether he wanted to or not. I got involved with the choir, and he sat in the congregation. We went to marriage Bible studies where we had the opportunity to interact and ask questions. In all this time, I was so excited in my newfound salvation as "wife" that I didn't realize that we were not growing together, especially not spiritually.

chapter 6

Dabbling in "Magic"

A S WE PROGRESS into my "self-found" salvation journey, it is very important for you to know that Scotty truly did love me. He wanted so much to be the man I thought he should be. He tried to shelter me, protect me, and most importantly never disappoint me. This is truly my version of the story with a self-righteous filter that would soon be shattered.

I started to realize something was wrong when he wouldn't let me see the credit card bills. Was he *dabbling in magic?* He would tell me he had bought me a gift and didn't want me to see what it was. Another surprise? I do love surprises! Was it a puppy? Was it a new car? (I got both!)

I had forgotten about the credit card statements until he started to travel with work. Of course, a statement arrived in the mail, and I saw that he was making phone calls with his credit card, not his calling card. However, being the trusting, redeemed wife, I simply asked him about the charge. He said I had been working so much that he got lonely. They were just "chat" lines where you talk about the weather and stuff. Please remember, just because I had sex, did not make me less naïve. I believed him. I believed him so much that I apologized for not being there for him and for not making him first in my life.

Then the phone bill came. Again, he was on a trip, and this time there were calls to Portugal. Portugal? I quickly called the operator to inform her that we knew no one in Portugal! She explained to me that they were 900 numbers routed through international lines so the company could charge more. I quickly replied to her that I was very aware of chat lines and I thought that was an awkward thing to do! She then informed me that they were erotic fantasy lines. I burst into tears and could not stop crying. The operator (now counselor) tried so hard to calm me down and asked if I knew who would do such a thing. In my mind I thought, *Yes! I even know exactly who it is!* I was lost. How could I ask him about this? I began to tear the house apart. I found magazines—not girls who like to chat magazines—but naked girl pornography. I thought I was going to be sick. I turned from wife into CSI and found pornographic videos hidden with our Bible lecture tapes. (He did love theology.) I don't think I've ever cried so hard.

I put the videotapes on the dinner table, and gingerly placed my wedding ring on top. I wanted him to know that I knew. He walked into the house and immediately fell to his knees and begged my forgiveness. I was too mad to even look at him. I no longer "had" to forgive him because I was his wife. He was going to pay for this! I was disgusted. Did he not know what gift I had given him? Was I that inexperienced or that horrible in bed that he had to seek fulfillment elsewhere? We had only been married for eight months!

chapter 7

THE CURE

L UCKILY, MY FRIEND had the perfect solution. We were going to go out and forget about everything. I was introduced to the world of "shots" that night. No, not wine coolers—the hard stuff, tequila, lemon drops, and peppermint schnapps. It was like candy to a broken heart. She was right; I forgot everything. To this day, I don't even know how I got home. Scotty left the next morning on another business trip, and I had the wonderful opportunity to experience my first hangover. The light hurt my eyes. Quite frankly, it hurt to breathe. His childhood friend (we'll call him Joey) called to check on me. I was really scared that something was wrong with me. I truly thought I needed to go to the doctor because I was hurting so bad. Joey was a hangover veteran; he advised me to take a shower and meet him to go get something to eat. He promised I would feel better.

I met him at the Irish bar for dinner. I think the first thing I ate was another "shot." I began to pour my heart out to him. I was so confused and wounded that I couldn't see straight. Joey felt it was only fair to tell me all their secrets. Boys-night-out with my husband consisted of strip poker with strangers that had been picked up at a bar. There were even "truth or dare" moments where Joey witnessed Scotty going into a bedroom with one of these girls. I hung on every word as I followed my first "shot" with another. What was wrong with me? Why would he do that? Was I not sexy enough? Pretty enough? I went through the whole list until finally I decided I had to prove to myself that I had power. I could seduce someone! I would show him.

One bar led to another. One shot led to another, and then dancing led to dirty dancing. With more drinking and low tolerance, I definitely needed a ride home. Luckily, Joey volunteered. He walked me inside my house to make sure that I was OK. At that moment, I had the power. I began kissing him. He said, "We can't do this…we can't do this," but I drunkenly assured him we could, and we did.

I woke up the next morning feeling worse than I did the day before. Joey was lying on Scotty's side of the bed. What had I done? "Get out! Get out! You have to go! I can't believe I did this!" Joey began to laugh and warned me that I hadn't seen the last of him. It had to be the last of him! My husband was coming home that day! I showered; I washed the linens; I vacuumed (I guess another CSI thing). I did everything within my power to make that house clean. I know it was a lot cleaner than I *felt*. Finally, my husband came home. I ran out to hug him. I just held him while he pushed me away. Did he know? He said he felt grungy and just wanted to take a shower. I could definitely relate to that one, so he did. We went to bed and made love.

I just wanted my life back. I could forgive Scotty, but I could never tell him about me. I was so willing to forgive just to dissolve my own guilt. If he didn't want to go to church, we didn't go. I dropped out of the choir. I never received a phone call from the church wondering where I was, but that was OK. They would probably be able to hear the adulteress tone in my voice.

chapter 8

REGRESSION

A
S BADLY AS I wanted things to work with my husband, there were too many broken pieces. Did he not know how confused I was? How exposed I felt? Joey started calling the house and hanging up if Scotty answered. After a while, I began to enjoy the attention—the attention I was no longer receiving from my husband. I felt alive, sexy, and wanted. I even began to write Joey love letters telling him how wonderful I felt with him. I would juggle my time between Joey and my husband, almost pleased that I had the best of both worlds. But it didn't last.

The guilt definitely consumed me, and I began to push away from Joey. The phone calls started again, only this time there were threats—blackmail threats. He said if I didn't meet him he would tell my husband everything. I panicked. I jumped into the car, now feeling trapped—trapped and an adulteress.

I felt so guilty I couldn't do it anymore. Finally, I had enough. I informed Joey that I would tell Scotty everything because my marriage was worth saving. The phone calls stopped. I never had to tell.

Scotty and I went on a much-needed vacation to Florida.

We seemed to really open up to each other once again. We talked about everything, and I mean everything. He revealed to me that he had been unfaithful several times. He told me more detail than I wanted to know, but oddly enough, I felt relieved. It was as if everything I had done was now OK. After all, he was doing it too. This was my opportunity to tell him about Joey. I don't know why I told him, but I did. He was furious. I kept telling him he was being unfair. He tried to call Joey, and he would not stop pacing. I tried to reason with him, to tell him that it was over and to let it go. It was unfair that he would be able to confront him, because his infidelities were in other states. I was forced to trust that they were done.

We returned home, and his first trip was to Joey's work. He tapped Joey on the shoulder and said, "I want the love letters my wife wrote you." Joey was floored to say the least. He could not believe that I had told him. It was later that I learned they had made a bet. Joey "bet" Scotty that he could have me. He won. My marriage lost.

We really did try to make things work, but our relationship was now tainted. We didn't know how to trust each other. We were desperate. I called my brother. My brother had been through a divorce; maybe he could help us. He asked us one simple question, "Do you love each other?" We couldn't answer. I think we did. When I look back, I know we did. Yet, we also hated each other. Something was wrong...something was wrong with me.

chapter 9

Two Blue Lines

To add to the drama and downward spiraling relationship, I took a pregnancy test. There were two blue lines. I called the manufacturing company, as one line was "light blue" and the other dark blue. They informed me that any line at all, no matter how faint, meant "positive." How could this be a positive thing? I could have appeared on *Maury* at this point; I did not even know who the father was. I had to tell my husband the news. I also had to tell him that I did not know if it was his or not. He looked at me helpless. Had we not hurt each other enough? What in the world would we do with a child? I did not even have a guarantee that I would have a husband. In my mind, I was about to lose everything. I no longer wanted Joey in my life, and this news would simply become another game piece to him. I went to my doctor and she confirmed I was pregnant. She gave me all of these wonderful baby materials, and I began to cry. My doctor (now counselor) tried to understand my sobs as I told her I did not know who the father was. I knew it could only be one of two; what were my options? Her response was that I could have a DNA test after the baby was born. That's it? That's my only choice? Did she not know that my future was hanging in the balance? That the marriage I was working so hard to save rested on the paternity of this child?

It is amazing how painful these words are—to read them and remember. Yet God still had a purpose. I would love to tell you that there was a reconciliation, that God came in and healed our broken home. The truth is that God was never the head of our home. My husband drove me to the abortion clinic, and I signed away the life of my child. I remember staring at the ceiling with tears streaming down my face. What had I become? I was so ashamed of myself. For the next week, I stayed in bed and cried. I hated myself. I couldn't call my parents. My mother would be destroyed. I was the "good child." How could this have happened to me, my marriage...my baby? *God where are you?*

For those of you who have been through this procedure, you may have to forgive yourself every day. The truth is I think about this unborn baby often. I have dreams about her (always a girl). Someday I want to meet her and just tell her how sorry I am and how selfish I was and how scared I was. When I look back, no matter how much I feared being alone or disappointing my parents, they would have loved that baby as much as they loved me. I was simply more concerned about how *I* would look and how *I* would reflect on them. *Lord, just let my baby girl know that I love her.* God did heal and restore my heart—later.

chapter 10

HELL, FIRE, AND BRIMSTONE

I WANT TO GIVE you just a few words of hope as we continue to the next mountain. You need to know that I never blamed God or the church for these circumstances, nor did I blame the devil. I was very aware of the decisions I had made. "Train up a child in the way he should go: and when he is old he will not depart from it." I knew what decisions I should have made, and I became very accountable to myself. Unfortunately, I was missing one piece of the puzzle—grace. No longer a virgin (two-fold), married and divorced; redemption was indeed nowhere in sight. I called my father for help. I cried, "Daddy, what can I do? How can I go back?" He replied with the most positive intent, "If you know to do right, and continue to do wrong, there is no sacrifice left for your sins." My fate was now sealed. I had not even told him about the unwanted pregnancy. Not only was the hope of renewal and innocence forever removed, God had clearly stated I was done. For those of you who understand grace, you must forgive these few moments of hell, fire, and brimstone, but that is all I knew.

With my hell-bound fate, I openly made choices with no regard for God. It was not because I did not believe in Him or love Him. I had whole-heartedly convinced myself that God was so disappointed in me, there was no act of repentance possible. Drinking would help for a few hours, and then I would complete the ritual of staring at the ceiling with tears streaming down my face. I couldn't tell my parents. They knew me as the "good child." I could not disappoint them; I had to protect them from the person I had become. I found refuge in the arms of one man and then another. This was no longer the innocent dating from my college years. I was "giving up the goods." I never allowed myself to love. Of course, it wasn't hard. I didn't even love myself. I had resorted to "bootie calls." I don't know what they call it today. The basic definition is this: with a percentage of alcohol in your system you become extremely uninhibited. This feeling *must* mean that you need intimate relations with a man who is treating you exactly as you treat yourself—like garbage.

It is easy to see that I was continuing in a downward spiral fast. I didn't care about myself. I had moved from Ohio to Tennessee, and finally to Arizona. I felt like I was the cliché sailor with a guy in every port. I discovered how alone I truly was, even when there was someone lying there beside me. Although I didn't acknowledge God's grace, He had protected me in so many situations I put myself in. I was never raped. I never became pregnant again. I never contracted a sexual disease. *Lord, thank you for believing in me even when I didn't believe in You (or me).*

I would love to tell you that this part of my life passed quickly, but it took ten years. I used men, just as they used me. Some of them even fell in love with me. I just couldn't love them back. You can't love someone who doesn't love herself. I relied on alcohol to keep me from "thinking" about every bad decision I had made.

I didn't consider myself an alcoholic because I also poured myself into my work. I wanted to be the best and the brightest. Even today, I struggle with work/life balance, but back then, the only person I had to take care of was me (and my guilt). I worked as many hours as I could. I played as hard as I could. I worked out at the gym as hard as I could. All of these things filled my time just so my mind would forget. My mom used to always say, "The hardest person to forgive is yourself." It's true. The once beautiful, fun, church girl had turned into a party girl. Not even God knew who I was, at least that is what I thought.

chapter 11

TURNING THIRTY

I T WAS 1999, and I was about to turn thirty. This seems like fifty in girl years, that is if you are not married, engaged, or have a baby on the way. I began to get very depressed. I was dating someone, but I knew he wasn't the one. We simply tolerated each other. We got along really well (when we weren't hammered), but he was definitely never going to consider marriage, at least not with me. Oh, and did I mention I was turning thirty? I was in a dead-end relationship, unmarried, no hope of marriage or engagement, and I was about to turn thirty. I just wanted to go home.

My mother called and asked me what I wanted for my birthday and I told her, "I want to come home." Home was still Germany at the time. I asked my parents if we could drive to France (where my mother's family lived) and spend my thirtieth birthday in Paris.

I went to Paris for my thirtieth birthday. It was wonderful. My parents showered me with love and attention—unconditional love. They knew who I really was, even if I had forgotten myself. We returned to Germany, and my mother was going to a Bible Study. I didn't want to go, but my mother asked if I would go with her. I said OK, even though in the back of my mind I was thinking, "I need a drink!"

We arrived at the chapel. The book they decided to study was *Lord, Heal My Hurts* by Kay Arthur. I couldn't stop crying. Why this study? Why now? I realized that I had never "mourned" the loss of Scotty. I never mourned my failures. I wasn't moving past them, I was dwelling in them. I was drowning in them. We got home and I just continued to cry. I called Scotty. I apologized to him for everything I had done and didn't do. I was sorry for expecting him to be so much for me. I had hung on to him for all of the wrong reasons. I asked him to forgive me and I forgave him.

Most of you may be hoping that this was the turning point! God came in and made it all better! No, not yet. However, God was doing something. While I was with my parents, I received an e-mail from a friend from work (Graham) saying that he missed my smiling face around the office. Graham was just a friend—a very nice guy, but just a friend. I replied with thoughtful consideration, "You mush!" Remember, I was very happily in a dead-end relationship going nowhere.

I returned home and quickly returned to the bar. I had been thinking way too much for the past few days, and it was time to stop thinking again. The good news is that Bible study became a seed that was planted in my heart. The bad news is it still took me a couple of years to get it together.

chapter 12

SECOND CHANCES

I HAVE BEEN BATTLING with how I can bring you into my point of restoration. I know many Christians love the feel-good-emotional-overwhelming moment with overnight transformation. Please understand, I would never want to limit God, but since I have been asked to be both honest and transparent, you should also know that restoration continues to be a journey. More importantly, I must choose daily to live a life of restoration. It does not mean I do not make mistakes, even big ones. It means eventually you forgive yourself (because God already has), you learn from your mistakes, and you move on.

My dead-end relationship ended, and soon enough I was in the arms of another man—my e-mail buddy, Graham. He was very smart, reserved, and somewhat shy, except when he had alcohol in him. Needless to say, we both relied on alcohol: for me to forget and for him to feel comfortable. To this day, I have no idea how God put us together. I just know I am so glad he did.

I wish I could tell you that I met him at church or that he prayed the sinner's prayer with me. Instead we met for the first time at a bar in a restaurant in Tempe, Arizona. I was hanging over the bar flirting with the bartender who lovingly would place the extra shot in my drink. Graham and I were together for a quite a few happy hours since we both worked for the same company.

It was just a matter of time before another breakup happened and Graham and I began to date. I wasn't sure if he was interested, so I did a small test. I walked him to his door and he kissed me (at least I knew he was interested). After receiving the green light, it was less than a few days later when I showed up at his home (uninhibited/drunk). I don't remember that night at all. I do remember waking up, wondering where my clothes were, and wondering what I had done with my very good friend! As I was panicking (and searching for clothes) Graham walked into the room and said, "Happy Thanksgiving." To this day, we celebrate Thanksgiving Eve as a personal moment.

I really did like Graham, so I began to lay down the ground rules: "You have to date me. You can't just sleep with me." No one else had those rules. A few days later, we went out on our first date. The dates continued, and before I knew it, we were in a full-fledged relationship. Graham was unlike any man I had dated. My relationships prior to him had been full of drunken decisions, arguments, and of course, jealousy. I began to question if Graham really even cared for me. What kind of relationship has no fighting, no jealousy, and no drama?

I had so many unhealthy relationships, my idea of a normal relationship was somewhat warped. More importantly (and this is where accountability comes in), I took a piece of each unhealthy relationship into this new one with Graham. This means every selfish behavior that I had experienced or exhibited came right into this drama-free relationship with me. Six months into the relationship, I told Graham I needed a break. I'm not sure what I needed a break from since it was drama-free, but I just don't think I understood how to have or maintain a healthy relationship.

Surprisingly, Graham gave me my break. I don't remember how long it was, but something pulled me back to him. After about ten months of dating, we started talking about marriage, and a couple of months later we were engaged. I began to feel guilty wondering if he really knew how damaged I was—me with the scarlet letter on my chest! Obviously, this was still not a point of "restoration" because I was just as volatile in this relationship as the ones before Graham. I was still trying to stir up drama any way possible. Yet, for some reason, he stayed.

We finally got married at Paris Hotel in Las Vegas. Before anyone becomes overly concerned with getting married in Vegas, remember, I am the one who likes the "fanfare," and Graham is the quiet one. The thought of greeting two hundred strangers and thanking them for attending our "celebration" was a little overwhelming for him. I already had the big wedding once, so I thought, sure. Paris, Las Vegas, it is!

After we married, I continued to stir up drama. I have to wonder if I was testing him the entire first few months of our marriage, waiting for him to hurt me like Scotty did. If I let my guard down and he left, then I would be the stupid one. And yes, it was all about the fear of being stupid. While I continued to stir up drama I also stirred up credit card debt. Graham was this amazing pillar of savings and investing, now married to a die-hard Reaganomics fan—buying now and barely paying later! About $26,000 in credit card debt later, Graham was no longer the quiet one.

We began to fight. I used every mature comeback in the book: "You're not the boss of me." "I hate you." "I work for my money too." "If you're so unhappy, why don't you leave?" I even spoke the "D" word—divorce. I knew how ugly divorce was, yet I was willingly heading down that path once again. We had only been married eight months, and we couldn't stand to be in the same room with each other.

chapter 13

FINALLY

WE WERE DESPERATE, so we did what most people do when nothing else is working. We decided to give church a try. We went to a few different churches, and since we both grew up in different denominations, we needed to find a church that we would both enjoy. Then we found it: Phoenix First Assembly with Pastor Tommy Barnett. I loved the music program, and the teachings were amazing. I was not sure how we were going to change our lives just yet, but for now we were just focused on doing the right thing.

Our fighting and my spending slowed down (notice I did not say stopped), but my drinking did not. In fact, it was our one-year wedding anniversary, and I walked into Sunday school class with a hangover. I stumbled to the coffee pot, and I even cut in line. Obviously, my restoration was going to take some time. Who goes to Sunday school with a hangover? A preacher's kid, that's who!

Before you are completely disgusted at my church behavior, consider this thought: our pastor recently did a sermon on "belong and then believe." That is exactly what we did. We started to belong, and then we started to believe.

So although a Sunday school hangover was not necessary, we kept coming to church. It was not hard for me to get back into church. It was still where I felt safe. Plus, with an auditorium that seats over seven thousand, no one would even know if I was there or not!

I was very wrong! Not only did we meet another couple at the church, but also they lived in our same neighborhood! We began to get grounded at church, and our lives truly began to change. We began to communicate about money and started on an eager path to become debt free. I would love to say that we got that unexpected check in the mail that took care of everything, but God had bigger plans. It took us four years of hard work, and more importantly working together to get out of the mess.

It was definitely not easy, especially for the spender (me). I wanted to celebrate every little victory including "not spending money" if I went to the mall. My level-headed-husband was simply thinking, "Stay away from the mall." The good news is we had surrounded ourselves with couples that encouraged us both in our marriage and the financial goals we had set for ourselves. We were in church every time the doors were open, not only to hear the amazing message, but to be with our friends who loved us (unconditionally).

So let's recap a piece of this journey. We found an amazing church with incredible friends who loved us in spite of our imperfections and gave us the same grace that Jesus gave us? With so much love and grace around us, it should be no surprise that we just celebrated our eight-year anniversary!

Our celebrations and struggles are new every year. I have

learned that in a journey of restoration there are daily decisions that you make. Today, I choose to love my husband. Today, I choose that there will be no deal breakers for this marriage. Today, I choose to forgive the friend who hurt me. Today, I choose to make good financial decisions. Today, I choose to forgive myself. Today, I choose. The important thing to know is that the decisions "to choose" need to become a daily habit.

It's too easy to get sucked into a selfish society that dictates looking out for number one. Oprah and her generous giving should be the norm, not the exception. A successful fifty-year marriage should be the norm, not the exception. A strong, vibrant child that is eager to make a difference in this world should be the norm, not the exception.

If I have learned anything in my life, I have learned: I will always be judged by others, I will potentially always have enemies, and I will possibly be tempted by something bigger and better.

But today, I choose to be OK with who I am. I choose to thank God for everything I have. I understand that He has always had a greater purpose for me. Today, I choose to share that purpose with you.

Grace, Grace

As I see the world around me
And decisions that I made
My heart is full of wonder
I must be such a disgrace...

As I try to pick up pieces
Full of doubt and shame
I cry, "Lord please help me"
As tears stream down my face...

And then I hear, "Grace! Grace!
My child Grace! Grace!
I have always been beside you
I am here for you through Grace!"

I continue on a journey
Bound to fail again
Full of disappointment,
Hurt and self-blame...

My heart is clearly broken
As I struggle through my days
What have I done to myself?
Lord please change my ways!

And then I hear, "Grace! Grace!
My child Grace! Grace!
I have always been beside you
I am here for you through Grace!"

—PAULETTE LANGWITH

To Contact the Author

plangwith@hotmail.com